CW00349699

Music and Meringues on th

Music, food, family, friends and boats on and a

It's hard to say what we most like about the Isle of Bute. Perhaps the boats, or the sea, or our friends who come sailing over from the mainland. Maybe it's the music: the jazz festival, the open air services at the ruins of St Blane's or the live bands and solo artists in the local bars. It's certainly the trips on the Waverley paddle steamer – and the days out to Tighnabruich and to the Mull of Kintyre.

I think it's the miscellanea of silver and pink evening skies, Victorian architecture, happy memories, sandy beaches, basking seals, countless birds, wild flowers and picturesque walks: combined with a plateful of Rothesay Bay langoustines and Loch Fad trout for supper. It's the shipwreck at Ettrick Bay. The sea front at Kilchattan Bay: where my father, James Ekron Little, lived as a boy. And Rothesay: where my father-in-law, Stanley Morrison, was brought up in Battery Place, with his eight brothers and one sister. All wonderful singers.

Whatever that magic ingredient is, we love it so much that we've been coming back for over 40 years to work and holiday on this most glorious west coast Scottish island. Whenever we get a chance, we train, plane or drive up north, and board a ferry at Wemyss Bay for Rothesay. The minute we step onto the boat, a delicious lethargy envelopes us and we know we're back where the weather changes from blustery to sunny, to rain, to golden, in the space of an hour.

We love the lightness of air, and the lightness of being on the Isle of Bute. I expect you do too.

Mary Ekron Morrison
Isle of Bute, 2007

Left: I am in love with this ship-wrecked boat. It sat on the beach at Ettrick Bay – a wonderful sight at any time of the day or night. We make a point of bringing our friends here: then into the Ettrick Bay Café for the best meringues in the world. Large, light, fluffy and filled with fresh cream.

Right: Friends over for the day on the good ship Struan (centre left), leave harbour to sail back to Largs. It's been a glorious day and we feasted on langoustines from Rothesay Bay, local strawberries and cream, and wine from the Struan's store cupboard.

On a day like this, when being indoors is very tempting, it's lovely to wrap up warmly and walk along to Rothesay harbour to see who's in port. I spot the paddle steamer Waverley's funnels: grab a hot chocolate from Blethers café, and wander over to look at this most fascinating boat.

There's always something to stand and stare at. Best done with a bit of millionaire shortbread from one of the local cafés. I have a gold star award system for shortbread: and also for 'tablet' – that deliciously decadent Scottish fudge that melts in your mouth and rots your teeth!

Left: In the distance a liner glides down the River Clyde. From Greenock I expect. It looks quite surreal with the bus stop in the foreground and the little boats sitting in Kilchattan Bay. We are in the garden of St Blane's Hotel, with an evening drink. We watch the ship till it's out of sight.

Right: On our morning walk to Craigmore we stop to watch a two masted schooner making its way towards Rothesay. She's bound for the River Festival in Glasgow. Behind her, in the distance, is the Bute ferry heading for Wemyss Bay and centre left, the chimney at Inverkip.

Returning home after a day out on the Waverley paddle steamer, we meet the Glasgow sitting in Rothesay Bay. Our captain suggests we dance and sing and enjoy ourselves like the girls on the Glasgow. We cheer him and them: and have some good-natured banter between the two boats.

The three masted brig Jeanie Johnston in harbour. A stunning replica of the original 19th century sailing ship, which took passengers over from Ireland to America. On board is a famine history museum. She spent a few days at anchor locally, then off to the Glasgow River Festival.

Left: Easter Sunday I went to church and was given a great bunch of delicious smelling daffodils.

The nets on the harbour side looked so beautiful: but it was tricky taking the picture one-handed, with the wind trying to tear the daffodils and Sunday newspapers out of my other hand!

Right: A tradition dear to all seaside resorts. But a particular treat in Rothesay, where we swither between a single nougat at the Bay Café or a 99 at Zavaroni's. They do a great bacon buttie here: inside on a chilly day – and outside when the sun's around. And a sterling cuppa tea too.

Café ZAVARONI

Freshly Made Ice Cream
(Carry Out)

Cones	20p	90p	£1.60
99's	£1.00	£1.10	£2.00
Wafers		£1.10	£2.00
Nougats		£1.10	£1.30
Oysters		£1.20	£1.40
Sponges			£1.20
Marshmallow			£1.30
Top Hats			£1.60
Tubs		£1.10	

This disused WC always makes me chuckle. I imagine an estate agent's sign outside: 'For sale in convenient location. Great views. Fully tiled with multiple en suite facilities. Would suit DIY enthusiast with weak bladder. Or all round bird watcher.' It looks like a Victorian bathing station.

I love the outfits these two
are wearing. How elegant
and glamorous. That
turquoise waistcoat, and
those gloves! I am quite
envious and promise myself
to get dressed up for
next year's jazz parade.
I'm overdressed in an anorak:
but ready for the afternoon
jazz cruise.

Left: Here the great Jenny Brown leads the parade up towards the castle. There is such an air of happiness, laughter, friendly greetings to strangers and bon homie. The blue skies make a difference: there's no doubt about that. I finish the day covered in freckles and sunburn.

Right: Around the corner they go. By this time I'm dying of thirst and pop in to see Sue and John in Musicker, for a cappuccino and a large croissant. I am tempted by their books and music, and end up buying a Valerie Dunbar CD, in memory of my time working at West Sound local radio.

In July we spent our summer holidays on Bute – first stop a walk along the front at Kilchattan Bay. Behind us, in Surrey, we've left burnt grass in our garden, which we are unable to water because of a hosepipe ban. I admire this seafront garden and plan a similar change to ours.

It must have been the hottest day in the summer when we set out on our West Island Way walk.

Every step of the Way was a joy and a pleasure. The sea to the left of us, sun above us, flowers and bracken to the right, and surrounded by birds singing. The sea: picture book perfectly blue.

Left: MacCallum's Bay was crystal clear. A little boat sat at anchor. Apart from the call of the curlew, there was the most wonderful stillness and silence. Hard to imagine this was once a thriving port, with sailing boats bound for America. The ruins of the local inn now lost in the bracken.

Right: Following the path, we veered slightly inland and came across a lochan full of water lilies. I had a great longing for an iced coffee – but had to be content with some warm water from Brian's rucksack. And a bit of melted Kit Kat. I promise to bring a flask of ice, next time we go walking.

On we go, past Plan Farm and towards St Blane's churchyard where we walk round the moss covered gravestones and trace the dates with our fingers. There are a few tourists who've walked up from the road. We feel proud that we've come over the hill, on the ancient track.

After St Blane's the going gets harder with the sun beating mercilessly down and the path dipping and rising alarmingly. I wrap my cardigan round my head to keep the flies at bay. We're attracting quite a swarm of them. I expect we smell a bit ripe – and thus attractive to flies.

Left: We reach the highest point and start walking steeply down into the trees. Brian, slightly ahead of me, disappears into the foliage and I temporarily lose him. But I stick to the side of a dry stone dyke, which leads me to a stile, then welcome wooden steps: and back to the sea front.

Right: Brian takes a break on the nearest bench – and I stagger along to the post office for a reviving coffee. With my coffee, bag of Maltesers and newspaper, I sit munching and slurping happily while a young mother beside me watches her children playing on the rocks. An idyllic day.

An unknown couple, waiting for the Waverley paddle steamer to come round the corner on a hot summer day: for a trip up the Kyles of Bute and on to Tighnabruich.

People have been sitting on this bollard eating ice creams and waiting for the Waverley since time immemorial.

And there she is. Those distinctive funnels, the swollen belly, the pounding of the paddles. The gleaming engine room, handsome decks, good-natured crew, gentlemanly captain.

Part ship, part childhood memory. Perfect, whatever the weather. A ship for all seasons.

At Tighnabruich most of the passengers leave the boat for a visit to the nearest tearoom. The trick is to judge the time nicely for returning on board. Otherwise you'll be one of the stragglers getting cheered back on – as you run along with your wobbly bits bouncing.

Left: Down below us it's quiet and calm now that the engines have stopped their noise. A man and a dog on the wooden pier, keep an eye out on what's happening. I'm in photographic heaven – then realise I'm seeing everything through a lens. So just sit back and film it all with my eyes.

Right: On our wedding anniversary we decide to visit the Mull of Kintyre. First the ferry crossing from Rhubodach to Colintraive – then the drive to Tighnabruich. Splendid views. We pull in behind a shortbread truck from Aberdeen – to look in awe at the stunning Kyles of Bute and Tighnabruich.

This is what life's all about. A gently rocking boat. Peace all around. Beautiful views. Calm murmuring of the waves. Stunning colours and a good companion. What could be better? Obviously I'd prefer to be a stone slimmer and a bit more glamorous. But – so what!

Back at Rothesay pier, the fun begins as hundreds of us stream off, after our day trip. And hundreds stream back on board – after their day in Bute. This poor soul must be roasting in his doggie outfit. He has to ditch his cans of beer. It would never do to have a tipsy pooch on board.

Left: Another day we head on to Portavadie on the mainland, where we wait for the ferry to Tarbert. The sea, as so often on this coast, is sparkling clean and clear. Loads of mussels. My mouth waters at the thought of them cooked in wine, with chopped onions, garlic and tomatoes.

Right: We have a perfect time visiting Carradale and the Mull of Kintyre. Sea to the left of us, highland cows and wild flowers on the right of us. This is one of these roads that ought to be in a book of 'Places to see before you die'. Tarbert in the evening sun looks sultry and enigmatic.

And then a lovely evening sail across the water back to Portavadie. We watch a fishing boat – surrounded by gulls – making for Tarbert harbour. How peaceful this all is – the quarrel quite forgotten. Didn't I mention the quarrel – and the wasp sting? Immaterial now. All in the past.

Back home, we wander along the front – past the Cabbies' Rest. I'm always impressed by the hanging baskets and flowerbeds along the front at Rothesay. We enjoy the last of the sun – then to the Indian Restaurant for some vegetable pakoras and lamb madras. Yummy.

Left: This board, along the front at Rothesay, marks the Highland Fault Line. On one side of the board you are in the Highlands. On the other side – in the Lowlands. I jumped from side to side once or twice – but didn't feel any different. Apart from a different pic on the other side.

Right: There is a kind of music in the sound of the waves, the murmur of the wind, the rustle of the grasses. Sunday, Ettrick Bay – and apart from a mother and child off in the distance – the beach is deserted. It's a tad chilly. We walk smartly into the café. Soup and meringues for us!

After an 'all churches' open air service at the ruins of St Blane's church, up on the hill, we drive back to Rothesay. A spectacular sky marks the end of a deliciously languid Sunday. Now we're heading for the Golfers' Bar where Elvis McCartney is to be singing. An indulgence indeed.

We first heard the famous
Elvis McCartney (far left) at St
Blane's Hotel. He's got a vast
repertoire of songs – and
writes his own material too.
Here some friends join in and
jam with him. I love this about
Bute: the Jazz weekend,
Bute Live Festival and
constant occasional music.

Left: Arriving at Wemyss Bay for the ferry over to Rothesay: we feel we're really on holiday when we see the Victorian railway station. There was a time we used to wheel Bobby in his red pram, with a suitcase on top of the pram, onto the ferry: for a week at the Waverley Guest House.

Right: On a drive round the island with Stuart and Marjorie Young (over for the day from West Kilbride) we stopped to take a pic of the entrance to Kerrycroy. I realised my eyesight was less than perfect when Marjorie pointed out that the 'poppies' I like – were in fact marigolds!

And round to the white horse Brian loves so much. It promises to bring us luck throughout the holiday. As indeed it does – I've never known such a time for grand weather, good food, happy day trips, stunning walks and great pics. Pure magic.

Another tearoom, which serves up sumptuous meringues. Particularly handy as it has bus stops near by. We walk one way – then bus back if we're too full of pastries and delicacies. It's open occasional evenings too.

Left: The wonderful Isle of
Bute Discovery Centre.
The best tourist information
centre in the UK: bar none.
We pour over the old
photographs looking for
Brian's grand-parents. As
a young man, Brian's father
Stanley used to sing with
his band here and play the
cornet. Great cinema too.

Right: The evening sun hits
the side of Rothesay Bay
where Brian, as a boy used
to visit his aunt Margaret,
uncle John and cousin
Kathleen. Weather permitting,
we sit on a bench outside
their old home, with
a picnic of dressed crabs
and wine: and toast the
Morrisons, the Littles and
happy memories on the Isle
of Bute.